Victorian and Edwardian
BEDFORDSHIRE
From Old Photographs

1 St Paul's Church, Bedford, in 1859. This is the oldest known photograph of the county town, taken when scaffolding (right) had been erected for an extension to the Grammar School in St Paul's Square

2 *Overleaf* Jane Cirket of Elstow, a photograph taken in the 1850s. Note the supporting clamp, necessary to maintain the pose during long exposures, behind the subject's left arm

Victorian & Edwardian

BEDFORDSHIRE

From Old Photographs

Introduction and commentaries by

RICHARD WILDMAN

B.T. BATSFORD LTD

LONDON

For my parents

By the same author
BYGONE BEDFORD – A collection of 163 pictures (White Crescent Press, 1974)
BEDFORD PAST AND PRESENT – A collection of photographs of Old Bedford with present-day comparisons (Paul Hooley & Associates, 1975)

First published 1978

Filmset in Monophoto Apollo by
Servis Filmsetting Ltd, Manchester
Printed and bound in Great Britain by
Cox & Wyman Ltd, Fakenham
for the publishers B.T. Batsford Ltd,
4 Fitzhardinge Street, London W1H 0AH
ISBN 0 7134 1026 4

CONTENTS

ACKNOWLEDGMENTS

The Author and Publishers are grateful to the following for permission to reproduce photographs in their possession or custodianship: Mr C. Foskee Abraham (39, 74); Bedford Central Library (20); Mr Richard Smart of Bedford College of Higher Education (55–57); Mr John Turner and Miss Jane Hassall of Bedford Museum (24, 35, 91, 128); Miss Margery Brown (81); Mr Donald Chapman (21, 22); Mr and Mrs Alan Cirket (2, 49, 50, 99, 101); Mr Geoff Dillingham (70, 71, 80); Messrs H. F. and R. G. Gale (36, 52); Mr Bob Geary (17, 59, 114); Miss Margaret Gosling (16, 69, 87, 113); Mr Richard Hutchins, Clerk of the Harpur Trust (105); Mrs Clare Fleck and Mrs Marian Nicholls of Luton Museum (4, 9, 10, 18, 26–29, 32, 40, 47, 54, 64, 67, 68, 85, 96, 102–104, 109, 116, 120, 125); Mrs C. F. Mackay Brown (82, 115); Mr John Mathers (94); Mr Albert Moore (76, 122); Mr Stephen Nicholas (43); Mr G. D. Gilmore, former Archivist of North Bedfordshire Borough Council (3, 53, 108, 110); Mr D. M. Rump (95); Mrs Elsie Rump (60, 118); Mr Michael Rutt (75); Mr C. W. Saunders (77, 86); Mr Roland Scanes (37, 38); Mr Frederick Sharp (30); Mrs Judy Smith (88); Mr David Stonebridge (90); Mrs Joyce Wakefield (11); Mrs Olive Watson (130); Mr Terence Wells (106); Mr S. Williamson (44); and Miss Patricia Bell, County Archivist, Bedfordshire Record Office, for all the remaining photographs, except 7, 25, and 98, which are from the Author's collection.

The Author would also like to thank the following for their help in the preparation of this book: Mr Christopher Carter; Mr F. G. Cockman; Mr Denis George; Mr M. Gurr; Mr Bob Irons of Luton, photographer; Mr Nicholas Pemberton; Mr Ken Whitbread and Bedfordshire County Council photographic unit; the staff of Bedfordshire Record Office; and everyone who kindly lent photographs which it did not prove possible to use.

THE PHOTOGRAPHERS

The following Bedfordshire photographers are known to be represented in this collection:
Bedford: Blake & Edgar (35, 43, 60, 122); J. C. Brown (58, 73, 81); M. B. Dilke (17); G. Downes (42, 98); G. A. Gearey (34, 48); J. George (108); Kingham & Co (45, 52, 72, 88, 99, 126); D. Lindley (128); E. Walker (3, 124); B. Wiggins (25); *Dunstable*: C. Smy (78); *Luton*: F. Thurston (4, 27, 29, 40, 64, 67, 104, 125); *Potton*: G. B. Symonds (12); *Sandy*: A. E. Nicholls (86); *Shelton*: J. Robinson (127).

Two *London* photographers, Elliott & Fry (46) and J. Cruickshank Taylor & Sons (11) are also represented, together with W. & A. H. Fry (53) and A. H. Fry (44) of *Brighton*. The precise origin of the photographers J. Bishop (75); H. Robinson (87); and R. W. Stratton (76) is not known.

INTRODUCTION

The revival of interest in old photographs means that every part of Britain can now be seen to share in the visual record of the past. The camera is not only an impartial recorder; it is also omnivorous and undiscriminating, and can give to the apparently commonplace scene from daily life all the immediacy and – in retrospect – romantic aura which, before the invention of photography, were reserved for pictorial representations of well-known scenes of historical importance or impressive natural beauty.

Bedfordshire's scenery is, on the whole, unspectacular, and its place in the nation's history derives largely from the influence of a few great men – John Bunyan, John Howard the Philanthropist, Samuel Whitbread, William Hale White ('Mark Rutherford') – in the sphere of religion, literature, and ideas. But the landscape possesses many pleasant features, and several famous people, not even natives by adoption like John Howard, have been attracted to spend some time in the county. They include writers as diverse as Edward Fitzgerald, who stayed at Goldington Bury with his friend Kenworthy Browne, making frequent visits for fishing and contemplation to riverside inns such as the Falcon at Bletsoe, and Arnold Bennett, who wrote *Teresa of Watling Street* whilst living at Hockliffe from 1900 to 1903. Joseph Conrad, however, disliked living even for 18 months (from 1907 to 1909) at Someries Farm, near Luton. More recently, Robin Barrington-Ward, deputy-editor and later editor of *The Times*, had a week-end cottage at Swineshead (£60 a year) from 1940 to 1945. Fitzgerald's praise of the meandering Ouse in a letter of 1839 ('Here I am again in the land of old Bunyan, better still in the land of the more perennial Ouse making many a fantastic winding and going much out of his direct way to fertilize and adorn') is echoed by Hale White in his short *Life* of Bunyan (1905): 'The river all the way from the borders of Buckinghamshire to Kempston through Harrold, Milton (Ernest), Oakley and Bromham wanders through lovely meadows, often turning, after a course of miles, almost back on itself in order to get through the low hills, but near Bedford and Elstow, the land is flat, bare, and to most people uninteresting. Nevertheless it has its merits; a wide sky overhangs it, it is not intrusive, demanding admiration, and it is quiet.'

Bedfordshire's economy was predominantly agricultural up to and beyond the turn of the century, and it is this rural character which is represented by most of the photographs in this book. Farming and associated country crafts serving the great estates figure prominently, from the blacksmith and wheelwright (21, 22) to the rick-builder and miller (11, 16). The soil of mid-Bedfordshire is extremely favourable to market-gardening, which is still centred on the Sandy and Biggleswade area. Writing in the Edwardian period, C. Gore Chambers observed that 'it is not easy to draw the line very exactly in Bedfordshire between agricultural and market-gardening occupation. Many vegetables which were considered to belong exclusively to garden culture at the beginning of the nineteenth century are now cultivated over an extent of hundreds of acres, and garden produce is grown on small allotments, and on some of the fields of large agricultural holdings'. Just as the extension of the Midland Railway from Bedford to London in 1868 greatly stimulated the Luton hat-industry, so the existence of the Great Northern line passing through Sandy enabled Bedfordshire market-gardeners to supply London and the northern cities with fresh vegetables (and in return to receive valuable manure in the form of horse-droppings from the streets and stables of the capital). The scientific management of agriculture and horticulture was sponsored by the Dukes of Bedford on the Woburn Abbey estate, and in 1896 the County Council established an Agricultural Institute and Farm School on the Duke's land at Ridgmont, where some 20 pupils were taught farming theory and practice until the experiment was brought to an end by the disappearance (with the Institute's funds) of the council's Director of Education, Frank Spooner, in 1911.

In north Bedfordshire, the ancient craft of lace-making had provided in the eighteenth century a substantial cottage-industry by which women and girls could supplement a family's meagre agricultural earnings. The trade went into a steady decline from the 1830s, however, when competition from machine-made lace so depressed the hand-work industry that 12 to 14 hours of close work might earn no more than 6d, as recorded by Charles Freeman in his *Pillow Lace in the East Midlands* (1958). The 1901 Census lists 1,148 Bedfordshire lacemakers – most of whom would have been elderly – but attempts to revive the craft commercially in the late Victorian and Edwardian period met with some success (24, 25), and the skills are being fostered to this day.

Straw-plaiting (26, 27) for hat manufacture was the staple domestic industry in Luton and district throughout the first half of Victoria's reign, with 10,000 plait-workers in south Bedfordshire, according to the 1851 Census, although the arrival of much cheaper plait from first China and then Japan had killed off home-based plaiting by the end of the 1890s (28). However, Gore Chambers estimated that 'far more money is earned by the work of hat-making, trimming, and straw-dyeing, than was earned of old by plaiting', so Luton's prosperity continued to be sheltered by the hat. The actual making of the straw-hats and straw-bonnets was carried on in numerous small hat-factories (as well as some larger establishments) in the centre of Luton. A trade directory of 1906 lists 449 manufacturers of straw-hats and bonnets in Luton, only two of whom had already diversified into felt-hat making by which the straw-hat trade would be replaced after the First World War.

The story of photography in Bedfordshire is one of progress from obscure beginnings in the backrooms of chemists' shops to success by certain eminent local practitioners at the many international photographic exhibitions of the end of the century, together with occasional royal patronage. The earliest known photographer in the county was a chemist and manufacturer of false-teeth and soda-water, William Cuttriss of 64 High Street, Bedford, who left the town to practise near Leeds in the mid-1850s. Daguerreotypes by Cuttriss are said to have been extant in the 1890s, but none can now be identified.

As photographers multiplied following the introduction of the wet collodion process, the most eminent exponents of the art in Bedford were Arthur Maddison in the 1860s and George Downes in the following decade. The researches of Mr Denis George of Bedford have established that Maddison (1833–1887), the son of an upholsterer in Huntingdon, set up large studios first in Bedford at his home, 1 Priory Terrace, from 1862 to 1869, and subsequently at Huntingdon. He was a contributor to the letters page of the *Photographers' Journal*, in which he also advertised, claiming to have perfected an 'easy and effective' method of colouring collodion, for he saw himself primarily as an 'artist', at a later date even putting the words 'portrait painter' before 'photographer' in advertisements. He demonstrated his photographic method at a meeting of photographic societies at King's College in London in 1861. A trade announcement by Maddison in the 1870s declared that:

> 'Mr MADDISON is the only PHOTOGRAPHER in the COUNTIES of HUNTINGDON or BEDFORD whose Pupils have taken SILVER MEDALS in all the ENGLISH EXHIBITIONS. An assistant late in the employ of Mr MADDISON has since taken the HIGHEST MEDAL AWARDED at the PARIS EXHIBITION open to the WHOLE WORLD.'

Maddison took his stepson Frederick Hinde into the business, and in 1895 the latter opened a Bedford studio at Union Bank Chambers (20 High Street) under the name of Hinde & Carpenter, which was spread over the upper floors of the building in gilt brass letters. Despite a plethora of ingenious studio fittings and photographic equipment, described at great length in a local trade publication, where the firm also undertook to retouch and enlarge old photographs 'so faded as to be almost invisible', the Bedford business seems to have failed after a year or two.

3 One of a series of photographs by E. Walker commemorating Queen Victoria's Diamond Jubilee celebrations at Bedford on 22 June 1897. The photographer and his assistant standing at the foot of the Town Bridge (left) may have been employed by Walker

In the same year that Arthur Maddison left Bedford, 1869, George Downes ('photographer and artists' colorman, late Cundall, Downes & Co. Photographers to the Queen, 168 New Bond Street') purchased property at 72 High Street, Bedford, which he rebuilt and occupied until January 1879, after which his name is crossed through in the rate-books and Ellen Maria Downes (probably his widow) substituted (information from Mr Alan Cirket). Earlier in his career, Downes had photographed the *Great Eastern*, Brunel's great iron ship, under construction in 1855. Why he came to Bedford is not clear. His photographs, especially of individuals (42, 98) and groups are often encountered, and always convey that 'accuracy of character' and 'richness of tone' which impressed the *Bedfordshire Times* in 1874. As an example of the persistence of commercial goodwill in the photographic business, it is interesting to note that Downes's premises passed through the hands of four other photographers in succession: 'Monsieur' Joseph George (108); Drury Stowe; John Thomson (who also claimed royal patronage); and Ernest Swaine, until the connection was finally broken during the Second World War.

Another Bedford establishment whose existence spanned the last quarter of the nineteenth century and the first quarter or so of this century was Blake & Edgar, with studios successively at 32 Midland Road, 74 Midland Road, and lastly 38 & 40 High Street (from the mid-1890s). It is recorded that the wife of the founder of the firm thought 'Blake' by itself insufficiently refined and so, with Swan & Edgar in mind, the name of Blake & Edgar was adopted instead. Blake's son Ernest went into the cinema business in Bedford, founding Blakes' Theatres with his brother in 1897, and later became chairman of Kodak Ltd.

Meanwhile, in Luton, Frederick Thurston, FRPS (1854–1933), perhaps the most accomplished of all the county's early photographers, was reaching the heights of professional excellence. Thurston, who is shown with his family in 4, was born

4 The Luton photographer Frederick Thurston, FRPS (1854–1933), with his wife and children, Hubert (born 1887) and Muriel

in Luton and was probably apprenticed to a photographer named Henry Gregson, who had premises in King Street in the 1870s. Gregson or his predecessor, Samuel Debenham, took early views of Luton which were later absorbed into Thurston's stock. Thurston opened 'The Studio' as 'successor to Mr Gregson' in Hastings Street in or before 1885, and portraiture, especially of local civic dignitaries, was an early speciality, together with photographs of Luton industrial premises and their proprietors (29). Commissions from Madame de Falbe, lady of the manor of Luton in her own right, to photograph her guests at Luton Hoo (64) gave Thurston the opportunity to photograph the engagement of Princess Mary of Teck to the Duke of Clarence, second in line to the throne after his father Edward, Prince of Wales, which was announced from Luton Hoo in December 1891. Unfortunately, Thurston's hopes of a 'coup de photographie' were dashed when the Duke of Clarence's sudden death within a month rendered obsolete the stock of platinum prints of the engaged couple which Thurston had offered for sale at 7/6d each. The Princess subsequently married Clarence's brother, the future King George V, and became his consort as Queen Mary.

Like Arthur Maddison, Frederick Thurston was proud of his status as an 'artist', and won medals and distinctions at several international photographic exhibitions, in Russia and America as well as in Europe. Carefully-composed rural-idyllic subjects gained these prizes, whereas it is Thurston's townscape views which are more highly regarded today, such as the marvellous photograph of the timber-yard in Chapel Street, Luton (40), where the undulating railing of the Wesleyan Chapel is used to define the foreground, turning a fairly ordinary industrial scene into a picture of lasting quality and interest.

Little is known of the photographers who were active in the villages and smaller towns of Victorian Bedfordshire. Many seem to have set up shop in the great age of cheap portrait photography in the 1870s and 1880s, sometimes as a sideline to the trade of a rural chemist. William Fairey of Harrold is listed in a 1914 directory as 'draper and photographer'. Members of the Piggott family of Leighton Buzzard alternate in the directories as chemists and photographers throughout these decades. James Phillips of Shortmead Street, Biggleswade opened a branch in St Neots in Huntingdonshire in 1885, and an additional shop in the Market Square, Biggleswade, in the 1890s. The Potton photographer was George Symonds, who took the picture of Harry Kitchener's steam-binder *c.*1900 (12). Even a very small village like Tempsford on the Great North Road had its own photographer, Charles Litchfield, in the 1880s, though by 1894 he had moved to Ampthill.

The Bedford-born novelist William Hale White (Mark Rutherford) had his birthplace in mind when he wrote a series of novels in the 1880s depicting provincial life in a small town, variously named Cowfold and Eastthorpe, but unmistakably Bedford, on the borders of East Anglia and the Midlands during the 1840s, the period of his own childhood. In one of these novels, *The Revolution in Tanner's Lane*, published in 1887, he made the following observation:

> 'Many of us have felt that we would give all our books if we could but see with our own eyes how a single day was passed by a single ancient Jewish, Greek, or Roman family; how the house was opened in the morning; how the meals were prepared; what was said; how the husband, wife, and children went about their work; what clothes they wore, and what were their amusements. Would that the present historian could do as much for Cowfold! Would that he could bring back one blue summer morning, one afternoon and evening, and reproduce exactly what happed in Cowfold Square, in one of the Cowfold shops, in one of the Cowfold parlours, and in one Cowfold brain and heart. Could this be done with strictest accuracy, a book would be written, although Cowfold was not Athens, Rome, nor Jerusalem, which would live for many years longer than much of the literature of this century. But, alas! the preliminary image in the mind of the writer is faint enough, and when he comes to trace it, the pencil swerves and goes off into something utterly unlike it.'

As the photographs in this book show, photography was the medium which could fix the 'preliminary image' far more efficiently than the writer's pencil, and although Victorian and Edwardian photographs cannot tell us exactly what went on in the brains and hearts of Bedfordshire people in the nineteenth and early twentieth centuries, they enable us to make some excellent guesses.

RICHARD WILDMAN

Bedford, 1977

5 High Street, Elstow, looking south from near the Post Office (right), in the early 1880s. John Bunyan (1628–88), Elstow's greatest son, would have recognized all the buildings shown here. The medieval buildings on the left have recently been restored by North Bedfordshire Borough Council

IN THE LAND OF OLD BUNYAN

7 The Embankment, Bedford, looking west towards the Town Bridge, *c.*1890. The gabled building on the right is the Town and County Club (see 124)

8 The Square, Aspley Guise, in the 1860s

6 Statue of John Bunyan (sculptor Sir Joseph Boehm) on St Peter's Green, Bedford, shortly after its unveiling in 1874. The house on the left (7 St Peter's Green) was the residence of James Wyatt (1816–78), founder-editor of the *Bedford* (later *Bedfordshire*) *Times*, borough treasurer, antiquary and geologist

GLASS
EARTHENWARE

9 The fifteenth-century Market Cross, Leighton Buzzard, in the 1880s, flanked in this view by the Town Hall of 1851 (left) and the Corn Exchange of 1862 (demolished 1966), architects Bellamy and Hardy

10 George Street, Luton, looking north from the Corn Exchange towards the Town Hall. The Ames Memorial (see also 103) dominates the foreground of this photograph taken in 1886

FARMING AND RURAL CRAFTS

11 *Left* Hay-rick builders and rick-thatchers, with the tools of their craft, photographed at Great Barford in the 1880s
12 *Above* Steam-engine and binder at work in fields near Potton, *c*.1900. The owner was Harry Kitchener (standing, left)

13 Billie Wiggins of Pavenham, threshing beans with a flail, *c*.1892

14 Isaac Parker (right) with his threshing-tackle at work on Ben Jefferies' College Farm at Great Barford, *c*.1905. Parker was the village odd-job man, who had a special skill with machinery (see 72), and was said to have the power to charm away warts

15 Milton Mill on the River Ouse at Milton Ernest, designed in 1857 by William Butterfield, architect of Milton Ernest Hall, a few hundred yards upstream (see 66). Photograph *c*.1900

16 Joseph Cole (1811–89), miller, of Stotfold and Tempsford, photographed towards the end of his life. In 1859 he was an elector by 'freehold' at Stotfold and by 'occupation' at Tempsford. His grandson and two great-grandsons were also millers, at East Hyde, near Luton

17 *Left* Milking scene at Wilstead in 1911, with James and Frederick Quenby, two brothers who were small-holders and corn-merchants, and their house-keeper, Mrs Emma Inkersole

18 *Right* Joseph Fisher, a shepherd in the south of the county, who died on the last day of 1896 at the age of 85

19 A shepherd herds his flock through Elstow in the early years of this century – a scene which (like most of the buildings in this photograph) would have been familiar to John Bunyan. The shepherd's name was Cherry, and he lived in Bunyan's Cottage (demolished by the County Council in 1968)

20 The Bedford wool-fair was held on St Peter's Green on the first Tuesday in July, from its revival by George Hurst (see 126) in 1850 until 1872. This photograph was taken in 1864. The combined sign-post and lamp-standard (centre, left) marks the site now occupied by John Bunyan's statue

21 The old forge on Hogg Hill (now Brook End), Potton, photographed in the late 1880s, with the Fire Station, erected to commemorate Queen Victoria's Golden Jubilee in 1887, on the right

22 A wheelwright's yard in Bull Street, Potton, around the turn of the century

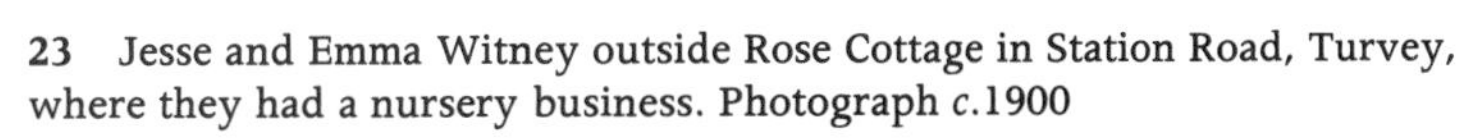

23 Jesse and Emma Witney outside Rose Cottage in Station Road, Turvey, where they had a nursery business. Photograph *c.*1900

24 All the implements of the lace-maker's craft are displayed in this obviously posed photograph taken in the early 1900s: the bobbin-winder (foreground); the pillow, and bobbins, resting on a three-legged pillow-horse (centre); and the flash-stool (right), into the top of which a candle-socket (or nozzle) was inserted. The light of the candle could be made to serve up to five lace-makers at once, by being refracted by glass globes (called flasks)

25 An elderly lace-maker at her cottage-door in the north of the county, *c.*1906. The pillow, on which the pillow-lace was worked, rests on a pillow-horse, and the bobbins were each weighted by a spangle of glass beads. The bobbins were often inscribed with names, including those of executed murderers, mottoes, or texts

COMMERCE AND INDUSTRY

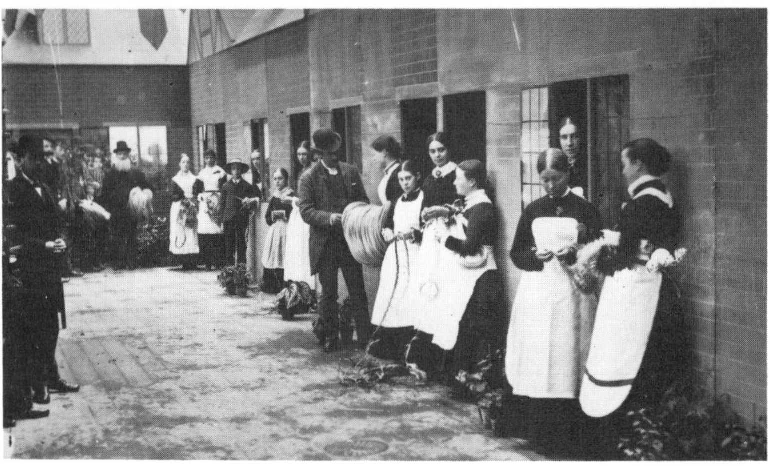

26 The old open-air straw-plait market in George Street, Luton, with the Town Hall in the background, photographed before the market was transferred to the Plait Halls in January 1869

27 Tableau at a trade fair in the Plait Halls, Luton, in 1887, depicting a straw-plait dealer bargaining for a coil of plait, to be re-sold to hat manufacturers. The girls are demonstrating the various stages in the plait-worker's craft

28 Bales of foreign plait, which have arrived by rail, being delivered to the factory of Richard Burley, straw-hat manufacturer, in Old Bedford Road, Luton, in 1909

29 In 1857, Thomas Sworder, a solicitor from Hertford, bought Burr's Brewery in Park Street, Luton, with all its licensed premises, for £41,250. Forty years later, having seriously over-extended himself financially in competition with J.W. Green, he sold out to his chief rival for £139,000

30 *Below* Brick-making at Cleat Hill, north of Bedford, in about 1906. The third man from the right was named Amos Fensome

31 A farmer engages two labourers on Dunstable Market, *c*.1890, whilst a delivery-boy smiles for the photographer

32 *Left* Chambers' general store was one of the block of buildings called Middle Row which stood on Market Hill, Luton, until its demolition by the local Board of Health in 1869. Frederick Davis (1816–74), shoe-maker and first historian of Luton, had the shop immediately to the right of Chambers' store

33 The premises of W. Francis, ironmonger and furniture-dealer, of High Street South, Dunstable, sometime in the 1890s

W. FRANCIS
LONDON, BIRMINGHAM & SHEFFIELD WAREHOUSE.
FURNITURE
BEDSTEADS, BEDDING, CARPETS, LINOLEUM,
MATS, MATTING, PICTURES, BASKETS, BOXES
LAMPS, CHINA, GLASS, EARTHENWARE
IRONMONGERY
BUILDERS & CARPENTERS TOOLS, SCREWS
NAILS, BROOMS, BRUSHES, PERAMBULATORS

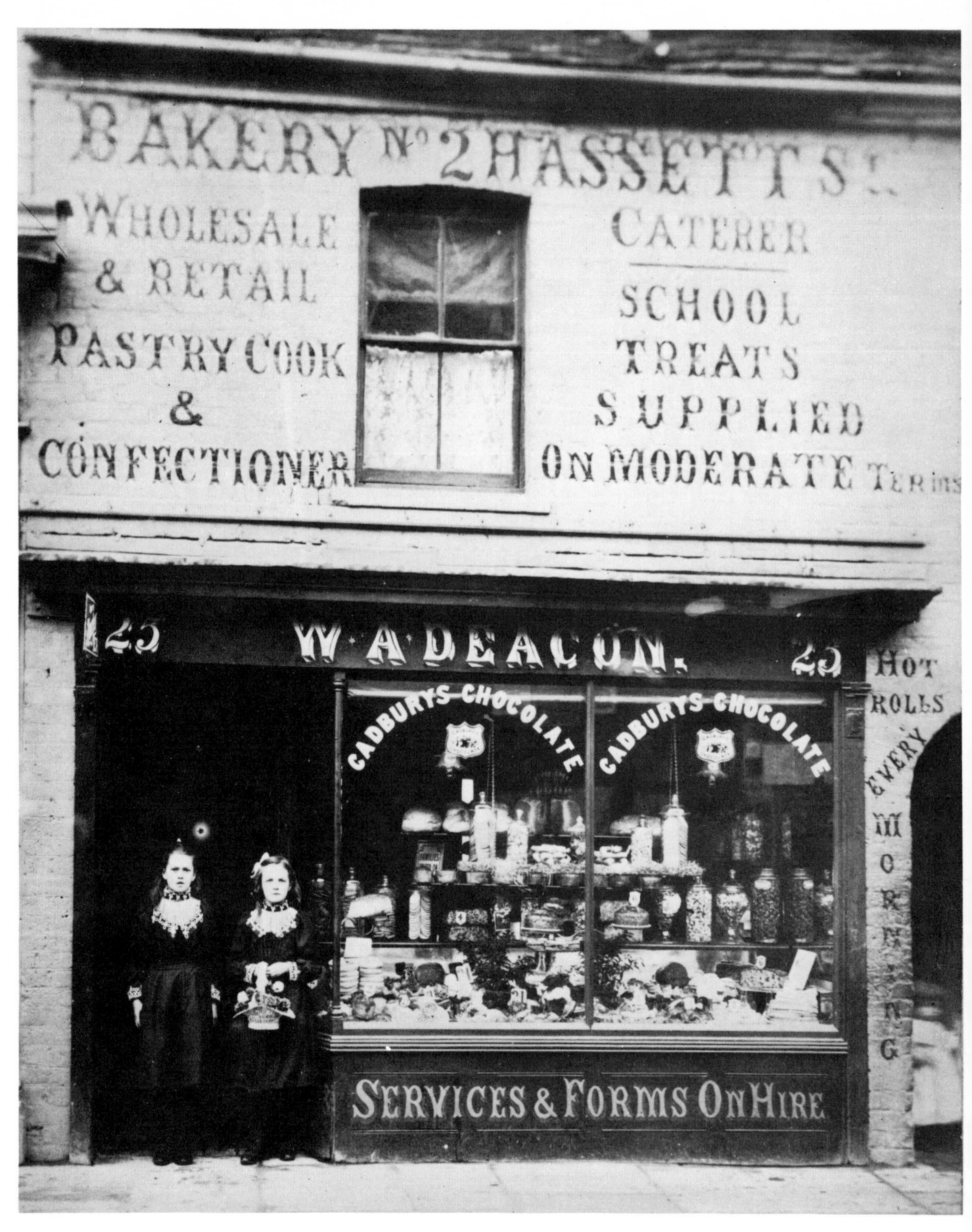

34 Annie and Margaret Deacon stand in the doorway of their father's sweet-shop at 25 Midland Road, Bedford, *c.*1905. On the right is the tunnel entrance to Christie's Court, which it was dangerous for the police to enter on Saturday nights, except in threes

35 *Above* Grocer's shop in the village of Bromham in 1906. A poster behind the small boy advertises the re-opening of the Royal County Theatre in Bedford on 6 August in that year

36 *Below* Rolls of wall-paper being delivered to Frederic Gale's premises at 3 Cardington Road, Bedford, in 1898. Frederic Gale (1867–1940) came to Bedford from his native Buckden in Huntingdonshire in 1889, and set up as a plumber and decorator. He was a deacon of the Mill Street Baptist Church (see 52)

37 George Kent Ltd, manufacturers of meters for water, gas, steam and oil, came to Luton from London in 1908. This photograph of *c.*1914 shows lathe-operators at work

38 Clerks in the office of George Kent Ltd of Luton, *c.*1914

39 The side entrance to Deane & Son's carriage works, of St Mary's Square, Bedford, was in Cauldwell Street, adjoining St Mary's Church Hall and Schools, which still stand, together with St Mary's Church in the distance. Photograph *c*.1910, as the business was sold to Nicholls & Son in the following year

40 Timber-yard at the corner of Stuart Street (left) and Chapel Street, Luton, taken from the forecourt of the Wesleyan Chapel before Chapel Street was widened in 1896 and the timber-yard removed

ESTABLISHMENT AND DISSENT

42 Rev. Henry Havergal (1820–75), Vicar of Cople from 1847 until his death, was a brother of the hymn writer Frances Ridley Havergal. He constructed organs at Cople and Willington churches

43 Rev. George Munby was Rector of Turvey from 1869 to 1905

41 Rev. Henry Tattam (1789–1868), a noted Coptic scholar who was Rector of St Cuthbert's, Bedford, from 1822 to 1849, and Archdeacon of Bedford from 1845 to 1866

44 *Left* The choir of St Paul's Church, Bedford, in about 1906, during the incumbency of the Rev. Lambert Woodard

45 *Below* The choir of St John's Church, Kempston, in about 1900, which included the present writer's grandfather, Bertram Howe (middle row, fourth from right), who later married the sister of Frederick Smith (front row, extreme right)

46 Three 'envoys' from Uganda, named Kataruba, Namkaddi, and Sawaddu, were brought to this countr in 1880 by the missionary son of the Vicar of Pavenham. They occupied a cottage in the village, until one bit off another's ear in a fight, whereupon they were sent home

47 *Above left* Members of the South Bedfordshire Clerical Society, photographed in about 1874. Their names and parishes were as follows: back row, from left, Messrs Southey (Woburn); Baker (Eversholt); Bradshaw (Billington); Veasey (Heath and Reach); Brickwood (Totternhoe); front row, Messrs Hamilton (Chalgrave); Gray (Hockliffe); Green

(Stanbridge Ford); Smythe (Houghton Regis); Hose (Dunstable); Hurnall (Eggington); unidentified; Cobbe (Milton Bryan); and Prescott (Caddington)

48 *Left* Dr John Brown (1830–1922), Minister of Bunyan Meeting, Bedford, from 1864 to 1903, and author of the standard *Life* of John Bunyan (1885), photographed shortly before his retirement. His daughter Florence was the mother of the economist John Maynard Keynes

49 Sunday School treat for children at Bunyan Meeting, Elstow, held in Mr Pestell's field, *c*.1906. Richard Poynter, for many years curator of the Bunyan Museum in Bedford, is the bare-headed figure with a moustache, holding up a little girl in the centre of the picture

50 The Methodist Chapel at Wilstead (built 1841), photographed in the 1890s

51 Laying the foundation-stone of the Wesleyan School in Dunstable, on 31 May 1909. Mrs Mark Guy Pearce is receiving the children's gifts

52 The Minister and Deacons of Mill Street Baptist Church, Bedford, in the early 1900s. This picture exemplifies the continuing Nonconformist influence on the business and public life of the town, viz: back row, from left, Messrs S.W. Leete (Bedfordshire County Surveyor); Frederic Gale (plumber and decorator); Francis Gamman (house furnisher), who was Gale's father-in-law; and Jones (foreman to S.W. Jarvis, stone-mason, who is first left in the front row). After the Minister, Rev J. Hobson Thomas, with glasses, come Messrs Lee (manager of Ellis & Everard, coal-merchants) and Lodge (manager of Forder's Brickworks at Wootton Pillinge, now Stewartby)

THE TEACHERS AND THE TAUGHT

53 The first reunion of Old Bedfordians (former pupils of Bedford Grammar School) was on 30 June 1880, when a dinner was held in the Swan Hotel, with Sir Erskine May, KCB, in the chair. Also present was Major Fred Burnaby (extreme right, second row from front), later killed on the Gordon Relief Expedition in 1885. The heavily-bearded James Surtees Phillpotts (1839–1930), Head Master from 1875 to 1903, stands at the apex of the group, beneath the 1767 statue of Sir William Harpur, who endowed the Bedford Charity (the Harpur Trust) in 1566. The former Grammar School is now the Old Town Hall

54 The staff of Waller Street Higher Grade School, Luton, *c.*1890. The headmaster, H.C. Middle (with beard), had been head of Waller Street School since 1884; it was turned into a Higher Grade School for boys in 1890, with fees of 7d a week

55 The staff of the Bedford Kindergarten School and Training College at 14 The Crescent, Bedford, in 1886: standing, Miss Birney and Miss Masters; seated, from left, Miss Wragge; Miss Sim (principal); Mrs Wodehouse and Miss Lewis. All except the principal were former students of the school, which had opened in 1882. Miss Wragge later founded the first free kindergarten for poor children in London, at Woolwich

57 *Below* Cardboard-modelling in the Bedford Kindergarten's preparatory school in 1901. Writing in the *Froebel Gazette* in 1897, Miss Walmsley, the principal of the training college, observed: 'It is astonishing to note the self-restraint imposed by these children upon themselves in the effort to perfect their handwork. Success in manual work gives the children that sense of power so essential to the fullness of life.' A pupil a few years earlier was Christopher Carter, 'Touchstone' of the *Bedfordshire Times*, who recalled in 1972 that, during the régime of the first principal, Miss Sim, 'all I learned at her kindergarten was to cut all manner of queer designs out of pink shiny paper, to keep my face and hands clean and my hair well brushed back'

56 *Above* Students of the Bedford Kindergarten Training College engaged in clay-modelling in 1901, with Miss Amy Walmsley, principal from 1896 to 1928, standing second from left, in a white embroidered smock with a bow at her neck

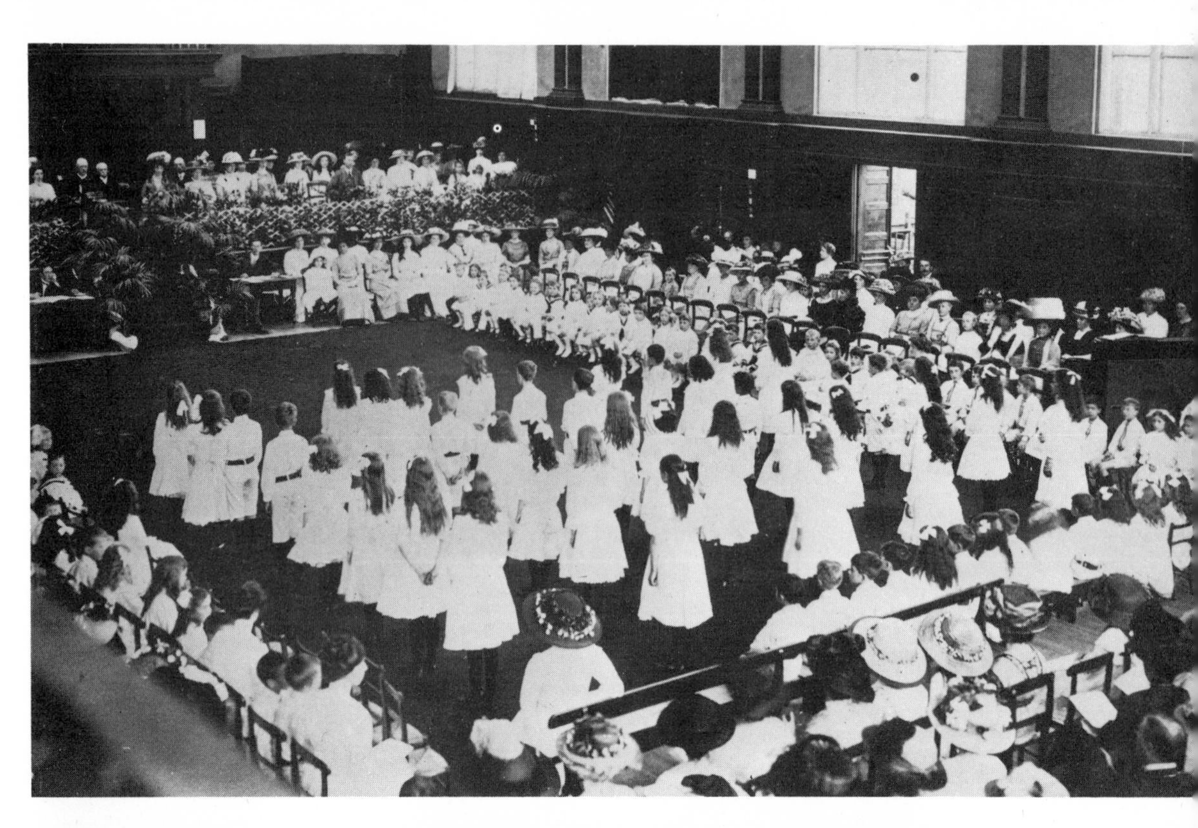

Wilstead
Infants

58 The annual Summer Festival of the Bedford Kindergarten School, *c.*1910, which was held in the Corn Exchange. The children are about to perform a folk-dance

59 Infants' class at Wilstead village school in 1897. The teachers were Miss Lavinia Smith (left) and Miss Henshaw (back row, centre)

60 Girls in Standard VII at the Girls' Elementary School, reached from an alley-way leading off Midland Road, Bedford, in 1906, when Miss C.A. Etchells was headmistress. Provided by the Harpur Trust until 1903, and thereafter by the local education authority, this school catered for the daughters of local tradesmen, who could compete at 13 for exhibitions to the Trust's Girls' Modern and High Schools. This picture was kindly lent by Mrs Elsie Rump (née Crawley), who is second from right in the middle row

ABOVE AND BELOW STAIRS

61 Croquet on the lawn at Box End House, Kempston, in the 1860s

62 The Hon. Eleanore Mary Rice-Trevor (1838–97), of Bromham Hall, daughter of the 4th Lord Dynevor and lady of the manor of Bromham

63 Miss Rice-Trevor chose a number of girls from the village Sunday School to be her attendants, on special occasions, and provided them with uniforms for use in summer (as here) and winter. The top-hatted figure is Harrison, her steward

64 Guests at a house-party at Luton Hoo, given by Madame de Falbe (1821–99), *c*.1886, with the Bishop of St Albans on the left. Madame de Falbe's second husband had been John Gerard Leigh of Luton Hoo, on whose death in 1875 she became lady of the manor for life

65 Scene at Sandy Lodge in 1899, on the wedding-day of Agnes, daughter of the 1st Viscount Peel, who had been Speaker of the House of Commons from 1884 to 1895

66 Milton Ernest Hall, built 1854–58, was designed by William Butterfield for his brother-in-law Benjamin Starey. From 1906 to 1919, the approximate period of this photograph, it was the home of Lord Ampthill, and is now an hotel and restaurant, having been completely restored in recent years

67 The funeral cortège of Sir Julius Wernher, Bart. (1850–1912) of Luton Hoo, a South African millionaire and lord of the manor of Luton since 1903, who died in May 1912

68 The south front of Luton Hoo in Madame de Falbe's time, *c*.1890, with her head gardener, Mr W. Perry, and his family in the foreground

69 Mary Ann Cole (1809–80), elder sister of Joseph Cole the miller (see 16), was born at Greenfield, where her father Charles Cole was a farmer. For several years she was a governess in the service of the Williamson family of Kempston Manor, later leaving Bedfordshire for Nottingham, where she died unmarried

70 Kitchen-staff at the Bedford County Hospital (now the South Wing of Bedford General Hospital), shortly after its opening in 1899

71 Three of the County Hospital domestic staff at Bedford, wearing their uniforms of starched white aprons and lace caps, *c.*1899

72 Isaac Parker of Great Barford (see also 14), with a knife-grinding machine of his own invention, *c.*1906

73 The oldest inhabitants of Thurleigh, *c.*1906, after a life-time of honest toil. Only the former postman (second from left) is not named; the others were (left to right): W. Darlow; Mrs Johnson; Mrs Hite (aged 94); Miss Smith; Mrs Hill; and Mr Hill

74 The High Sheriff's coach (and his trumpeter) outside the Swan Hotel, Bedford, *c*.1900. The coach was supplied by Deane & Son, carriage-makers, of St Mary's Square (see 39)

GETTING ABOUT

75 James Rutt (1838–1904) of Langford, pork-butcher, grocer, and soap-maker, known as 'Pimmy Pork', with his son Levi Rutt (1873–1965), later the village postmaster, photographed in 1895. In 1888, whilst apprenticed to a grocer in Islington, Levi had run all the way to Whitechapel to visit the scene of one of Jack the Ripper's murders

76 The yard of the Swan Hotel, Bedford, *c.*1906. The Swan's own horse-drawn omnibus (right) collected hotel guests from Midland Road station. The coachman was Frederick Moore (holding the lead horse's bridle)

77 'Large Atlantic' locomotive No. 1416 beside the Great Northern platform at Sandy Station, *c.*1908

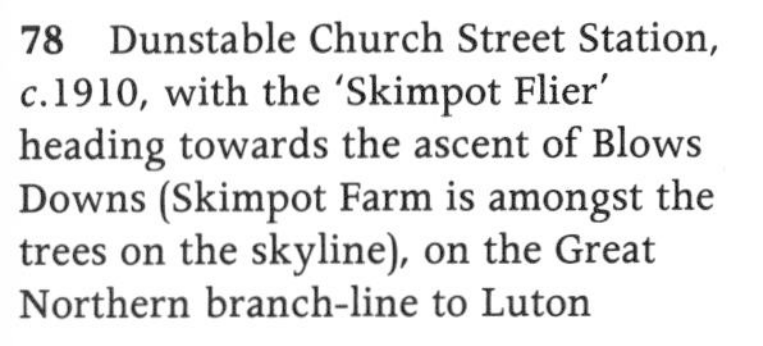

78 Dunstable Church Street Station, *c.*1910, with the 'Skimpot Flier' heading towards the ascent of Blows Downs (Skimpot Farm is amongst the trees on the skyline), on the Great Northern branch-line to Luton

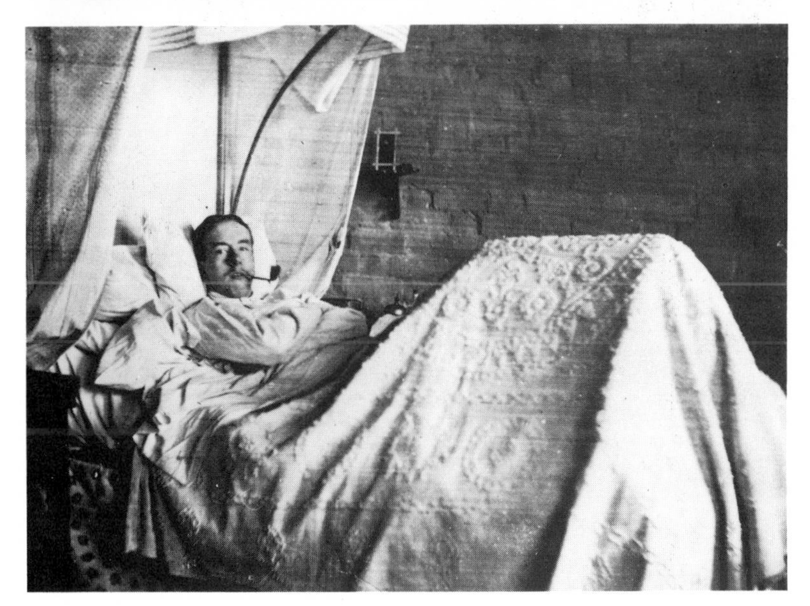

79 A survivor of the disastrous collision in Arlesey Siding on 23 December 1876, in which five people died

80 The messenger at Bedford County Hospital (successor to the Bedford Infirmary). posing on his official bicycle, *c.*1899

81 The Bedford photographer Jabez Charles Brown (centre) in the driver's seat of his $4\frac{1}{2}$ h.p. De-Dion *voiturette*, which he bought in 1905 and sold in 1909

82 Fitzgerald Verity Dalton (1862–1930), of Dean House, Upper Dean, with his wife Louise, daughters Charlotte and Margaret, and son Louis, in his daffodil-yellow 10 h.p. 1 cyl. Rex (known locally as 'The Yellow Peril'), 1903. He was one of the first car-owners in the north of the county

83 Car belonging to the Marquess of Northampton, in a ditch at Chalk Cutting, near Dunstable, following an accident on the evening of Monday, 19 October, 1908

84 Airship R31 on its maiden flight over Bedford in August 1918. It was the first airship to be built by Short Brothers at Cardington, near Bedford, but various faults caused it to be scrapped in February 1919, after it had flown for a total of nine hours

BLOTT
the Queen

WARS AND RUMOURS OF WARS

85 During the last 40 years of the nineteenth century, the Bedfordshire Rifle Volunteers assembled for an annual week of training in June, and the NCOs are shown here assembled in front of the ruins of Houghton House, near Ampthill, where the camp was held. This photograph was taken *c.*1869. The bearded man standing directly in front of the second column from the left, with his right hand against his chest, is Colour-Sergeant John Bull, head of the firm of Bedford jewellers of that name

86 The volunteer: Francis Woolhouse Saunders, in ordinary life the proprietor of a saddler's shop in Sandy, was a colour-sergeant in the Bedfordshire Volunteers, and saw 22 years' service. Photograph *c.*1900

87 The veteran: Tom George of Tempsford took part in the battle of Rorke's Drift (22 January 1879) during the Zulu War. In later life he worked in his aunt's coal-business and afterwards had his own market-garden. Photograph *c.*1890

88 Herbrand Arthur Russell, 11th Duke of Bedford (1858–1940), seated in the centre of the front row, with officers and NCOs of the Bedfordshire Regiment, *c.*1900

89 Kempston Barracks, built as the depot of the 16th Regiment of Foot in 1874–76 at a cost of £50,000, became the headquarters of the Bedfordshire Regiment upon its formation in 1881. This photograph was taken *c.*1900. Regimental use of the barracks ceased in 1958, and this striking range of buildings facing Bedford Road, Kempston, is threatened with demolition by the Ministry of Defence

90 Members of the Pioneer Corps of the 1st Battalion, the Bedfordshire Regiment, with the implements of their various crafts, photographed in India at the time of the Chitral Relief Expedition, North-West Frontier, in 1895

1 Bedford celebrates following news
f the Relief of Mafeking, which took
lace on 17 May 1900. The lady
rossing the High Street and carrying
folded parasol is Mrs Sophia Langley,
vhose husband, George Langley, was
master at Bedford Modern School
or 50 years (1855–1905)

2 The South African War Memorial
n front of the Swan Hotel, Bedford,
hown here on its unveiling by Lady
Cowper, wife of the Lord Lieutenant,
n 2 June 1904, commemorates officers
nd men of the Bedfordshire Regiment
nd local volunteer forces who died
uring the Boer War (1899–1902). The
iting of the statue gave rise to the
oke that the Swan must be the only
ub in England on which a soldier
urns his back!

93 The Doms family, refugees from the German invasion of Belgium in 1914, found shelter with Mrs Bradstow of Odell

94 Following the outbreak of the First World War in August 1914, detachments of the Argyll and Sutherland Highlanders were sent to Bedford for training before embarkation to France. Their presence in the town is remembered with affection by older inhabitants to this day. Here two sentries present arms outside 8a Bushmead Avenue

95 Shortage of manpower in the First World War was responsible for the employment of these women road-sweepers in Mill Street, Bedford, in 1916

HEARTH AND HOME

96 Members of two Quaker families in the garden of the Brache Mill, Luton, on 11 May 1865, the day after the marriage of George Price and Maria Laura Knight

97 The Gray family, of the White Hart, Ampthill, *c*.1895

98 John Lund, borough surveyor of Bedford during the last 30 years of the nineteenth century, photographed here with his daughter, then aged 10½, in August 1872

99 William and Frank Cirket, sons of William Arthur Cirket, builder, bricklayer and parish-clerk of Elstow, photographed *c.*1893

100 Three of the athletic Abrahams children (seen here at their home, 30 Rutland Road, Bedford, in 1903) were to have links with the Olympic Games: Adolphe (extreme left) was medical officer to the British Olympic athletic team from 1912 to 1948; Sidney (front row, right) was a competitor in 1908 and 1912; whilst Harold, here being carried by his brother Lionel (centre), won the 100 metres gold medal at Paris in 1924. All the children were educated at the Harpur Trust schools in Bedford. Inset, their father Isaac and his wife

101 George and Sarah Sharpe with their three sons, Wesley, Arthur, and Howard, *c.*1898. George Sharpe was the Wilstead postmaster

CIVIC AMENITIES

102 The old Corn Market House on Market Hill, Luton, in the year of its demolition, 1867. It was replaced by the Corn Exchange, which was opened in January 1869, and demolished in 1951

103 The Ames Memorial Fountain, familiarly called the 'Pepper-Pot', commemorated Lt.-Col. Lionel Ames (1809–73), of The Hyde, Luton, who had been high sheriff of Bedfordshire in 1865. It stood in front of the Corn Exchange in Luton from 1875 until 1925

104 A ward in the Bute Hospital, Luton, built by public subscription and opened in 1882 on a site presented by the Marquess of Bute's trustees. Patients were attended by their own doctors. In the picture, *c.*1882, are (left to right) Dr Pauli; Dr Daniel Thomson; Dr Horace Sworder; and Dr Simons. Behind them is the matron, Miss Babcock

105 The operating theatre of Bedford County Hospital, soon after it was opened in 1899

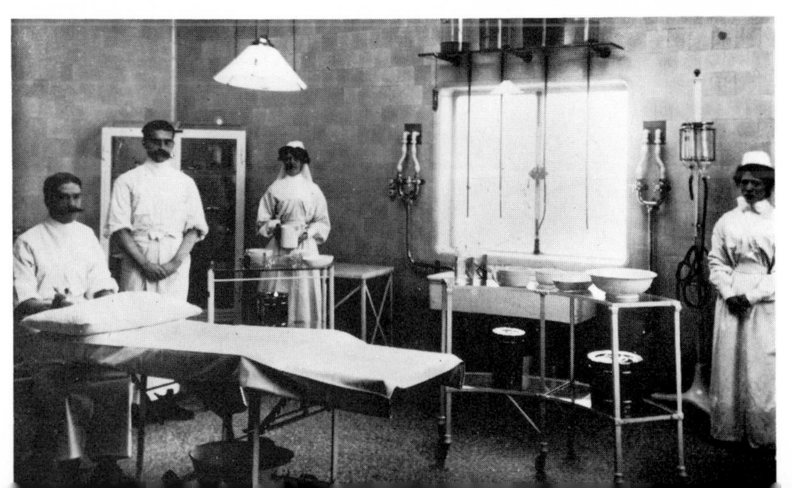

106 Sandy Fire Brigade, photographed in April 1894. Personnel included (front row, from right) Captain L. Hendry; 1st Foreman G. Haynes; and 2nd Foreman J.H. Mead

107 Shefford Fire Brigade outside the Jubilee Fire Station, about the time of its opening (1897). The engine was constructed by Shand & Mason of London

108 Prebend Street Bridge over the River Ouse in Bedford was opened on 21 October 1884 by Earl Cowper, the Lord Lieutenant, accompanied by such local dignitaries as the Mayor, Joshua Hawkins (with chain), and the M.P., the Marquess of Tavistock (in front row on dais, with dark beard). Earl Cowper stands to the right of the Mayor

109 The annual meeting of Luton's old Court Leet, originally the manor court, in the Corn Exchange in 1903. These meetings continued every Whitsun until 1939

110 Excavation work in progress during the construction of a reservoir for Bedford Corporation waterworks in 1912

111 Bedfordshire County Council road-repairing crew and steam-roller, early 1900s

SPORT AND ENTERTAINMENT

112 The Crown Inn, Bromham, with its last landlord, James Rust, and his family. It closed in 1904 and was demolished in the following year to widen the western approach to Bromham Bridge

MOTORISTS
CYCLISTS
ANCHOR
ACCOMMODATION
MARTIN GEORGE

113 The Anchor Inn, Tempsford, in the early 1900s, when the licensee was Martin George

114 Boxing Day rabbit-shoot at Dane Oak, Wilstead, in 1908. Taking part were, left to right, Charles Hebbes, owner of brick-kilns; George Geary, carpenter and undertaker; James Beagley, proprietor of a tailor's shop in Bedford; Reginald Hebbes, gardener; Rev. Richard Whitworth, Vicar of Wilstead; William Geary, son of George Geary; and George Warren, gamekeeper

115 J.W. Rawson Ackroyd (1854–1926) of The Grange, Upper Dean, in his unique wheelchair, specially designed for his shooting expeditions after an illness left him paralyzed. Those present in the photograph, *c.*1914, are (from left): Allen, gamekeeper; Robinson, coachman and valet; Rawson Ackroyd; Louis Dalton; and his father, F.V. Dalton (see 82)

116 The octet from Bone's Mandolin Band, founded by Phillip Bone, the proprietor of a music-shop in Luton (which still exists) around the turn of the century, when this photograph was taken

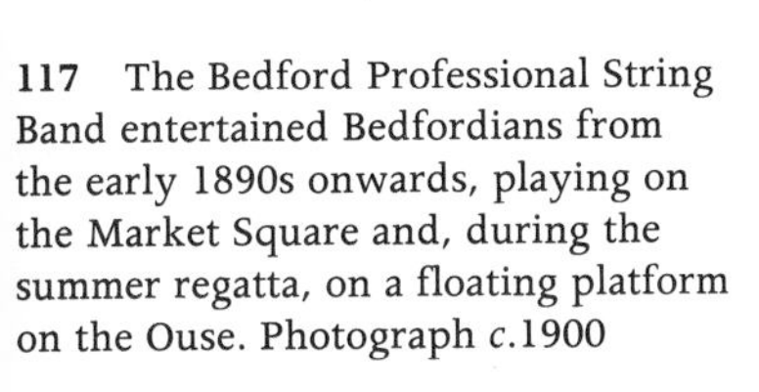

117 The Bedford Professional String Band entertained Bedfordians from the early 1890s onwards, playing on the Market Square and, during the summer regatta, on a floating platform on the Ouse. Photograph *c*.1900

118 Robert Holden Crawley (1864–1922), son of a Bedford ironmonger, was a champion local athlete in the 1880s, when this photograph was taken

119 The crew of a Bedford rowing four, with coach and cox, early 1870s

120 *Above right* Luton Town Cycling Club outside the London Road lodge (since demolished) of Luton Hoo, photographed by Frederick Thurston on 2 October 1886. The club had been formed on Easter Monday 1878, when 16 members set out to cycle to Bedford, and nearly half of them got there. It was in the 1880s that penny-farthings were being superseded by new models with wheels of equal size

121 *Right* Members of Clifton Cycling Club, photographed in the 1890s, by which time the invention of the lady's safety bicycle had enabled women to join these clubs, which had previously been male preserves

122 A meeting of the Bedfordshire Automobile Club outside the Swan Hotel, Bedford, in 1908. Lord Ampthill's car is the one with a roof in the front row

123 Col. Olliver Thomas Duke addresses an election rally outside the Swan Hotel, Leighton Buzzard, in the 1890s. Col. Duke, who lived at Heath and Reach, was the unsuccessful Tory candidate for South Bedfordshire in 1892 and 1895. Elections were a major source of public entertainment, and hotels still occasionally served as campaign headquarters

124 At the beginning of 1891 there were 13 weeks of frost, with skating, sliding and sledging on the frozen Ouse on moonlight nights until the small hours. Prominent on the left of this photograph, taken from the Town Bridge in Bedford, is the Town and County Club, designed by Henry Cheers and built in 1886. From 1956 to 1969 it served as the County Library; Bedford Corporation pulled it down in 1971

ROYAL OCCASIONS

125 The Duke and Duchess of Teck were among Madame de Falbe's regular guests at Luton Hoo, and in this photograph by Frederick Thurston, *c.*1890, they are shown with their daughter, Princess Victoria Mary of Teck (fourth from right among those seated on the steps), later Queen Mary (1867–1953). Her engagement to the Duke of Clarence was announced from Luton Hoo in 1891, but as he died soon afterwards, Mary of Teck married his younger brother, later King George V. In this picture Madame de Falbe is seated immediately behind and to the left of the Princess

26 George Hurst (1800–98), last urvivor of the unreformed (pre-1835) orporation of Bedford and ubsequently mayor five times, places is hand on the bell he gave to St aul's Church to commemorate Queen ictoria's Diamond Jubilee and his wn 97th birthday (10 February 897). The two other bells were given y Thomas Bull, churchwarden (first eft), and Sir Frederick Howard 1827–1915), co-founder of Britannia Vorks, Bedford, (second from left). he vicar was the Rev. Lambert Voodard, and the fifth man was robably a reporter

127 Almost the entire village was present at the Diamond Jubilee celebrations in Marston Mortaine on 22 June 1897. 500 dinners were served at 6d each, and 300 children had a free tea. The total cost, recorded by the Rev. Alfred Torry, was £43. 18. 4½d, leaving a balance in hand from subscriptions of £1 10. 4½d. The photograph was taken by Mr James Robinson, of Shelton

128 Roasting the ox in Bedford Park, during the celebration of Queen Victoria's Diamond Jubilee on 22 June 1897

129 The Swan Hotel's own float for a procession through Bedford in honour of the coronation of King Edward VII and Queen Alexandra in 1902

130 Street party held in Great Butts Street, Bedford, to celebrate the coronation of King George V and Queen Mary in 1911